Presenting:

SEEN GREEN?

THINGS YOU MAY HAVE SEEN THAT ARE GREEN!

WORDS & ART BY: BRIANNA DAVIS

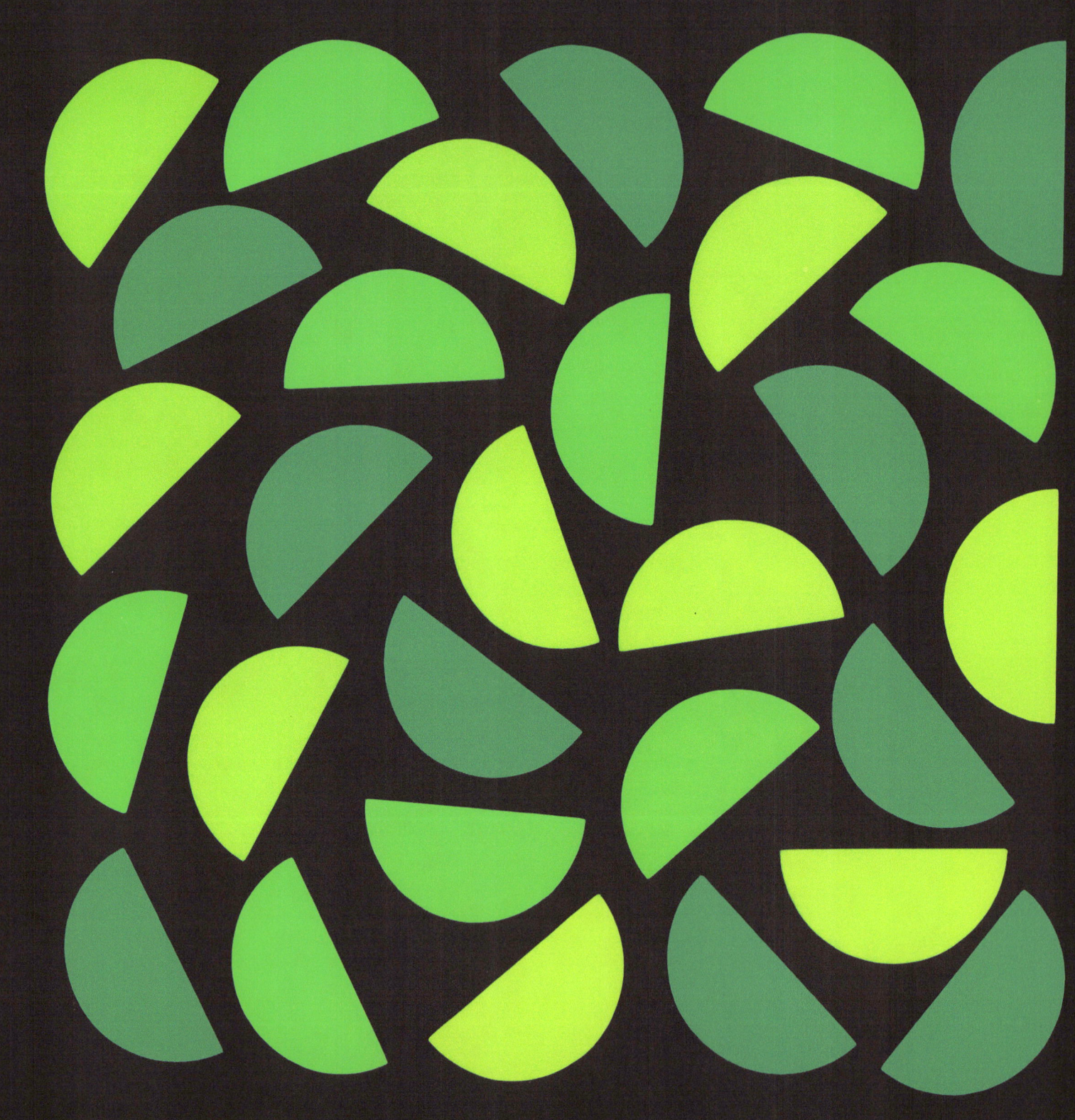

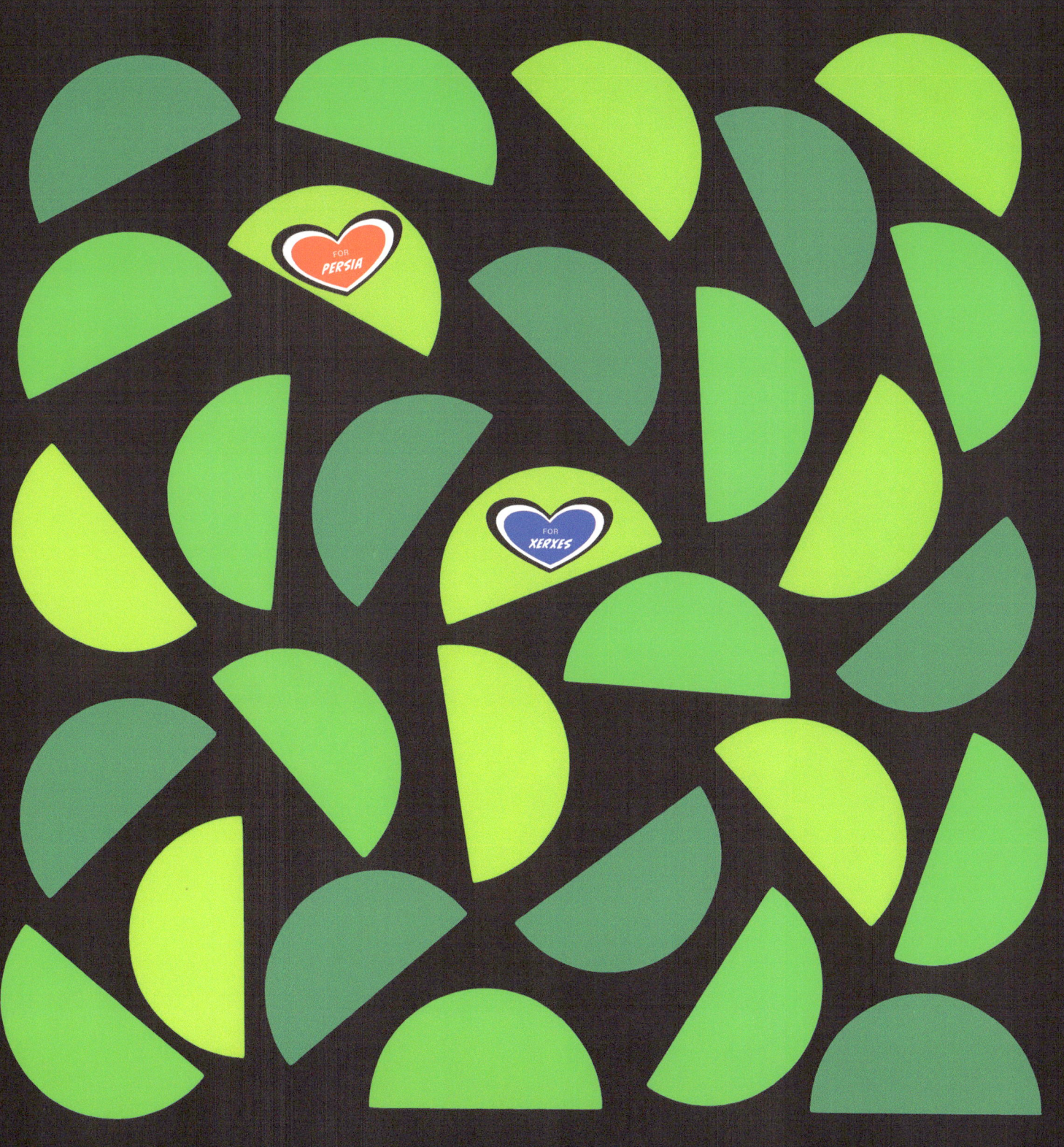

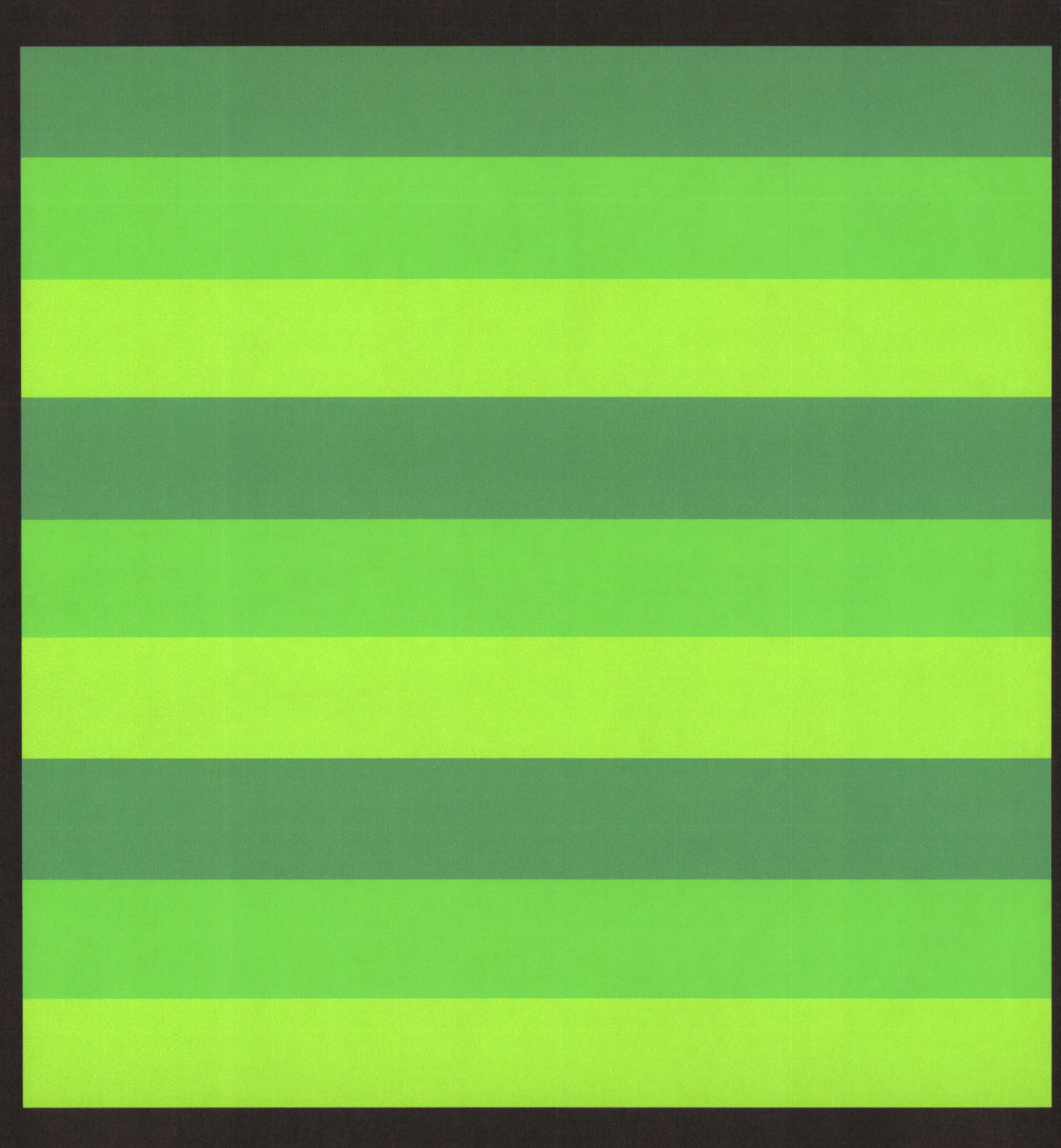

GREEN

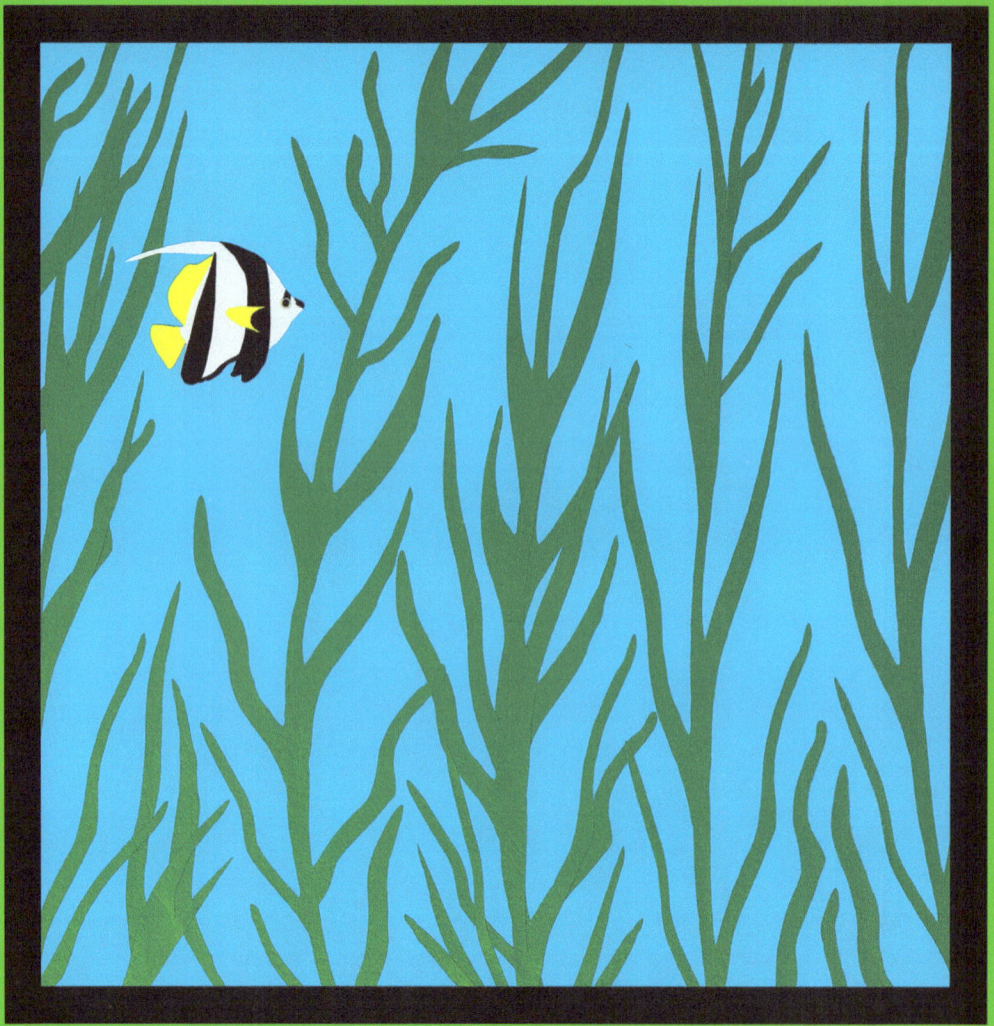

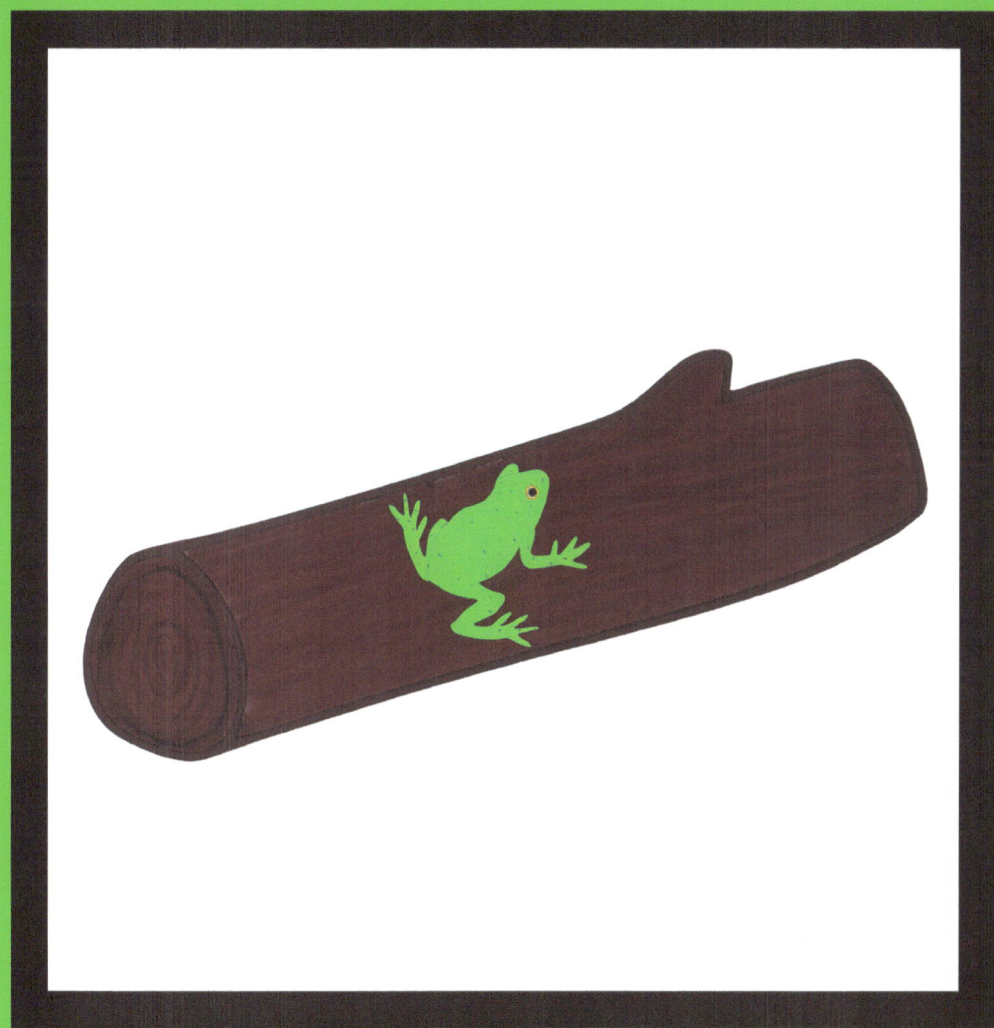

LOOK, THERE'S A FROG ON A LOG...

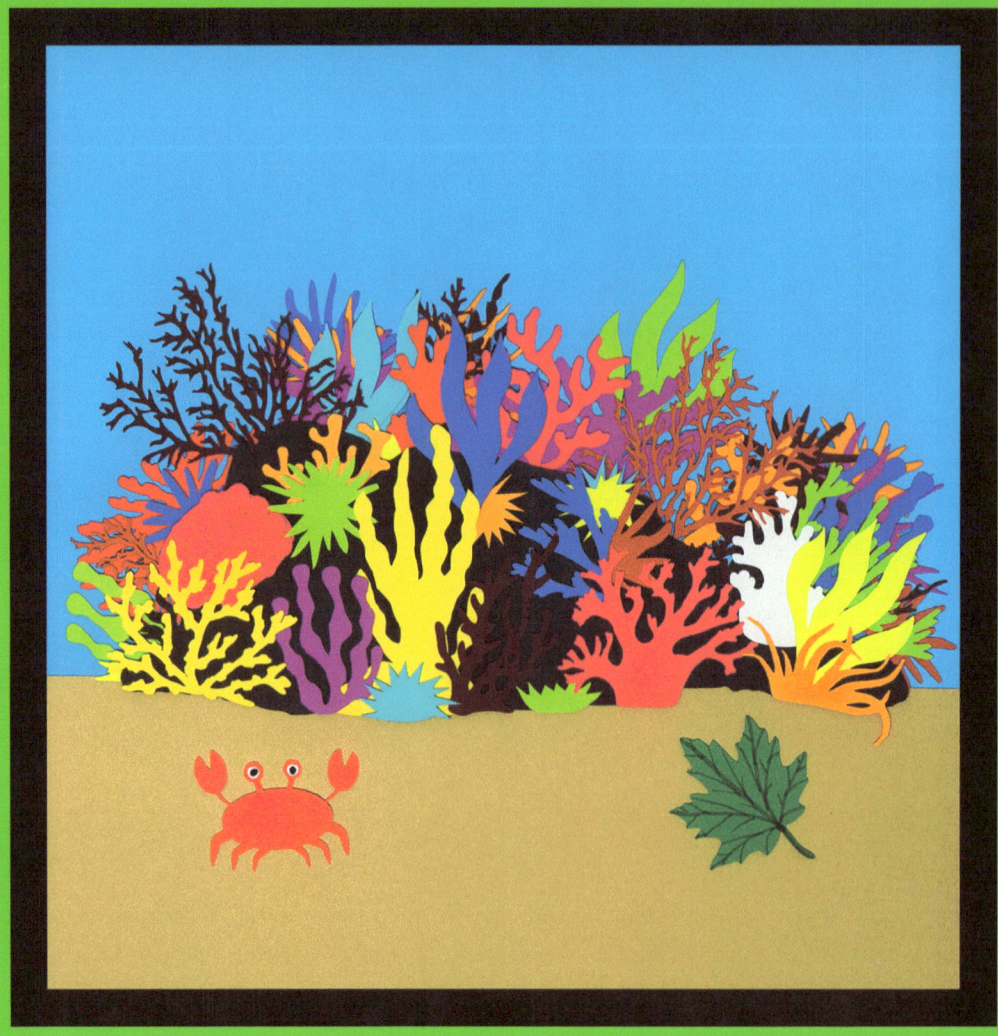

A LEAF NEAR A REEF...

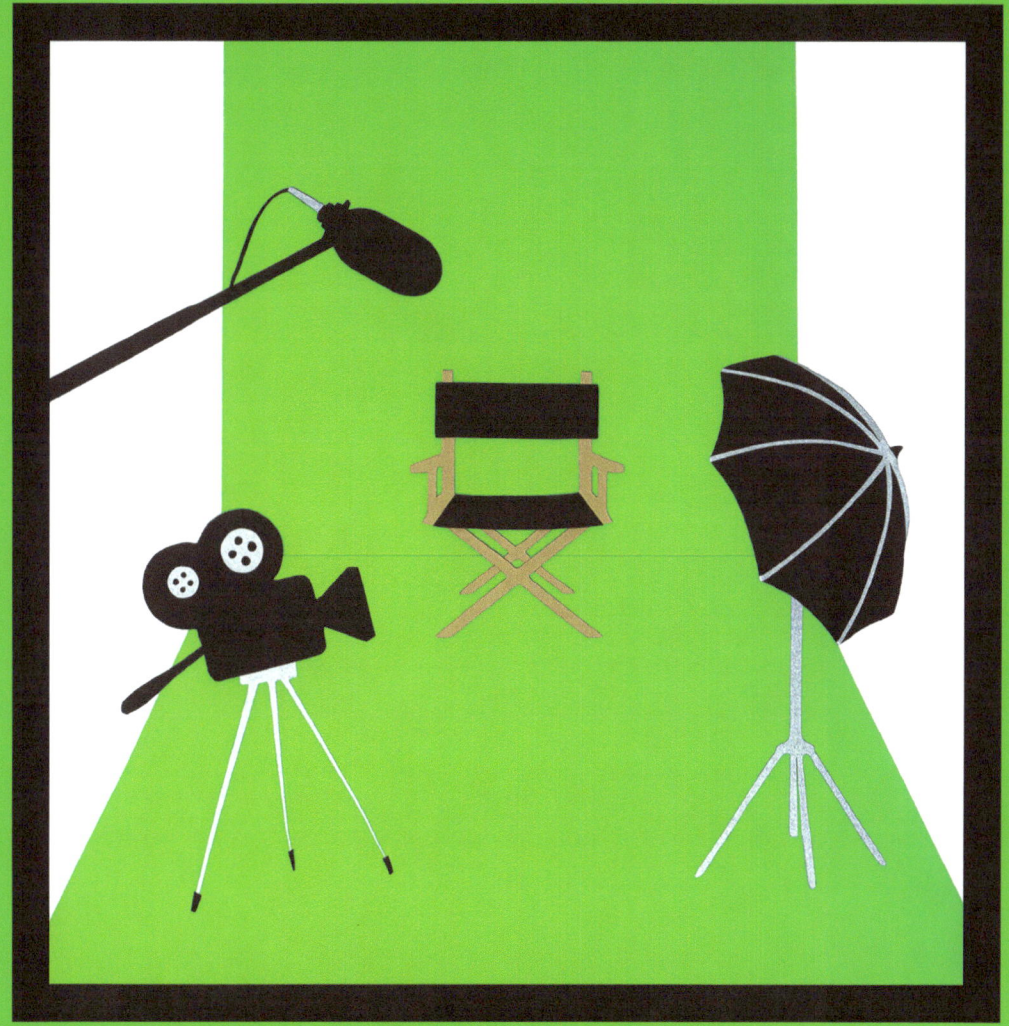

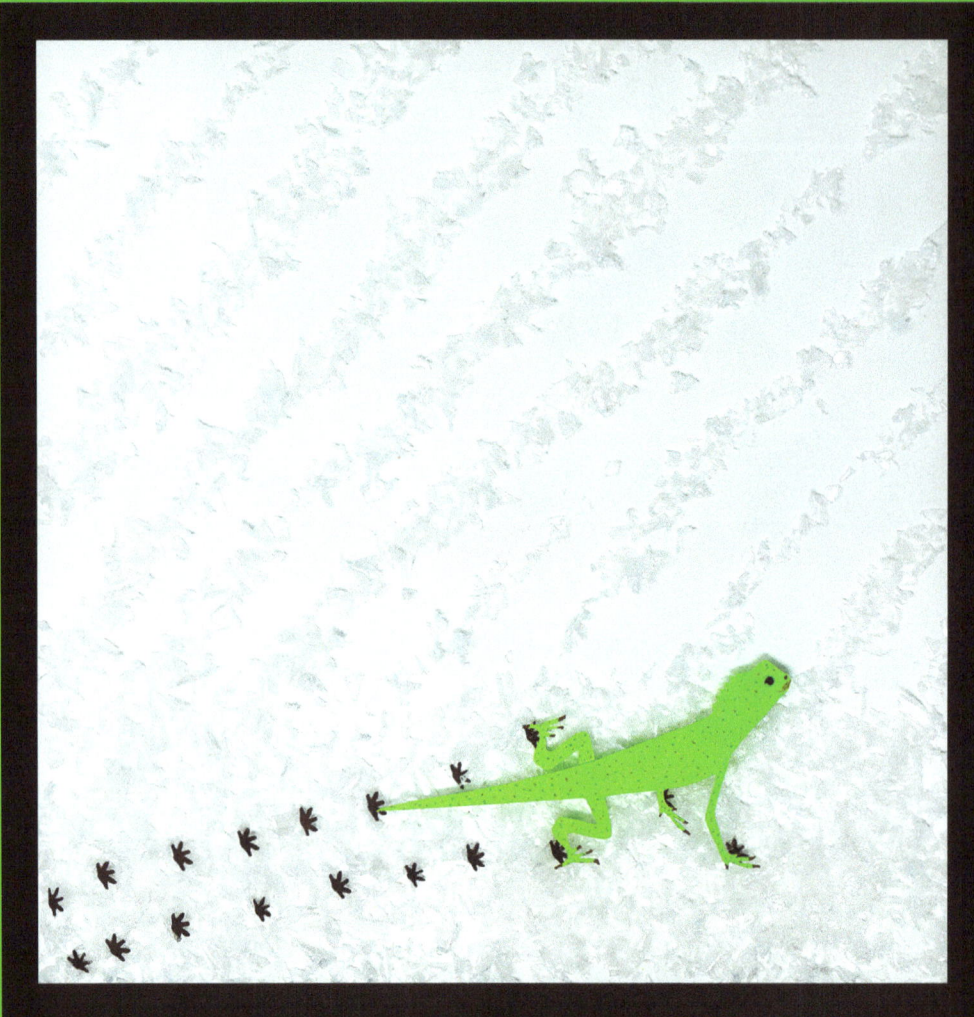

A LIZARD IN A BLIZZARD...

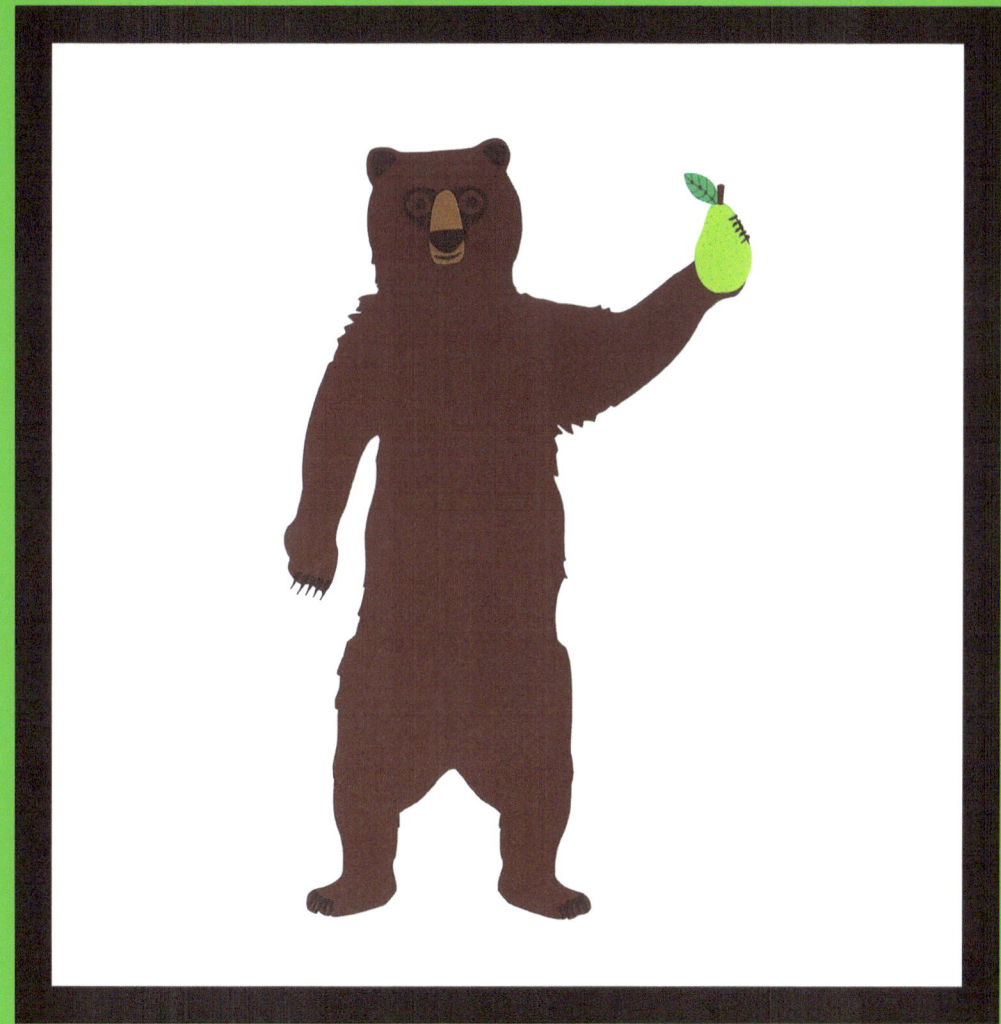

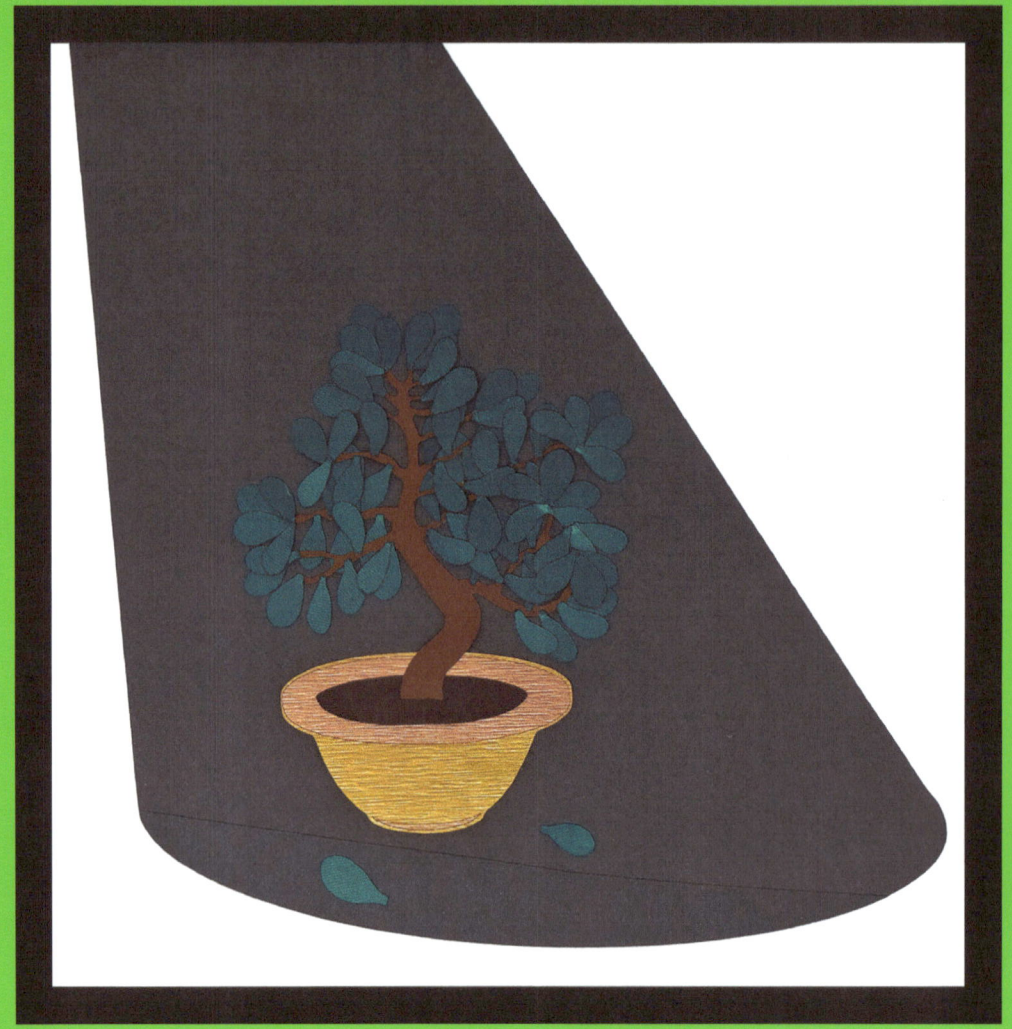

A JADE IN THE SHADE...

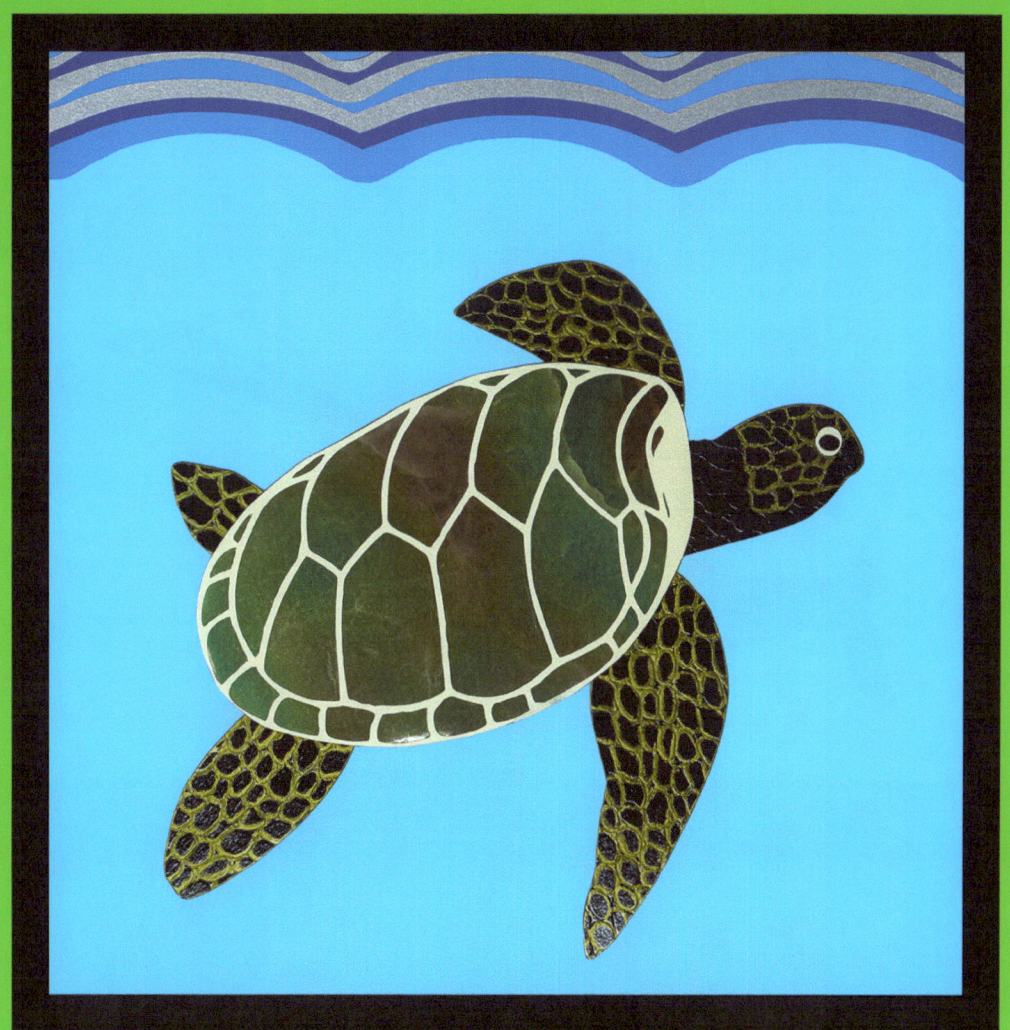

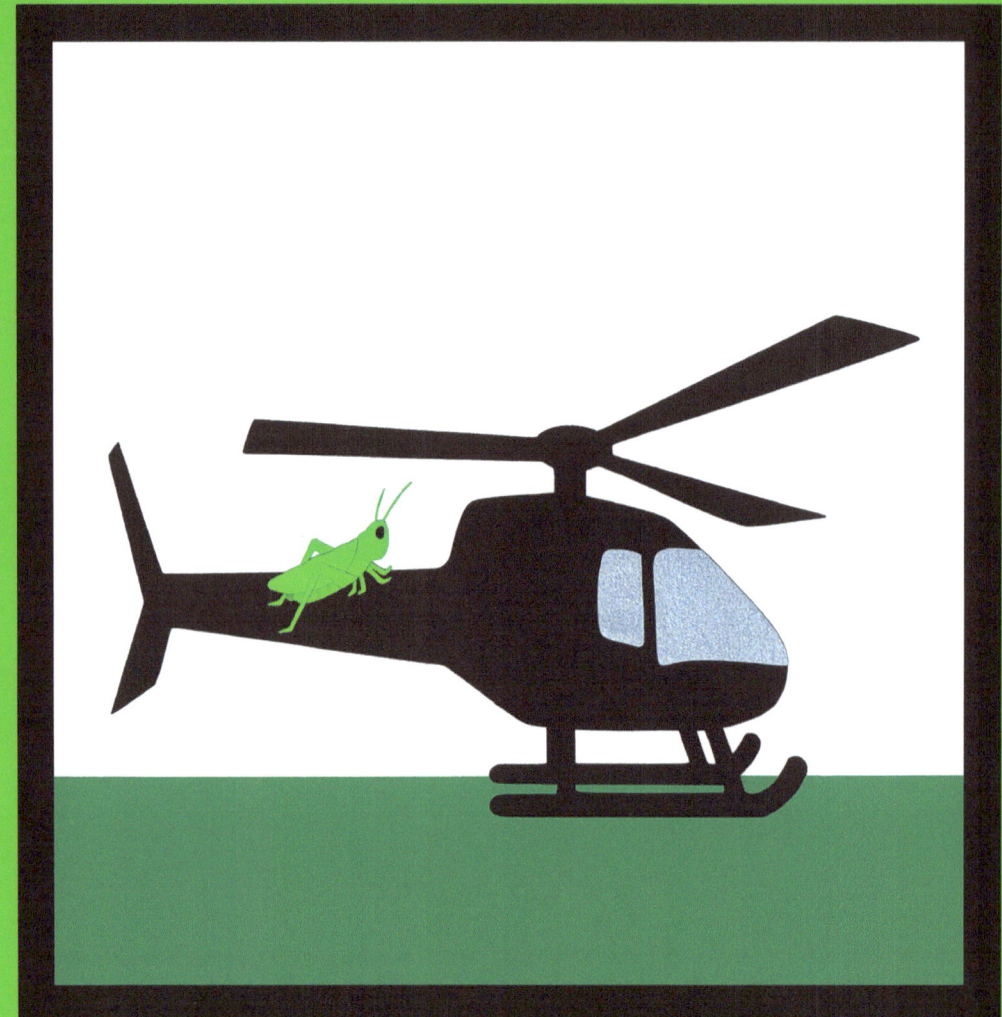

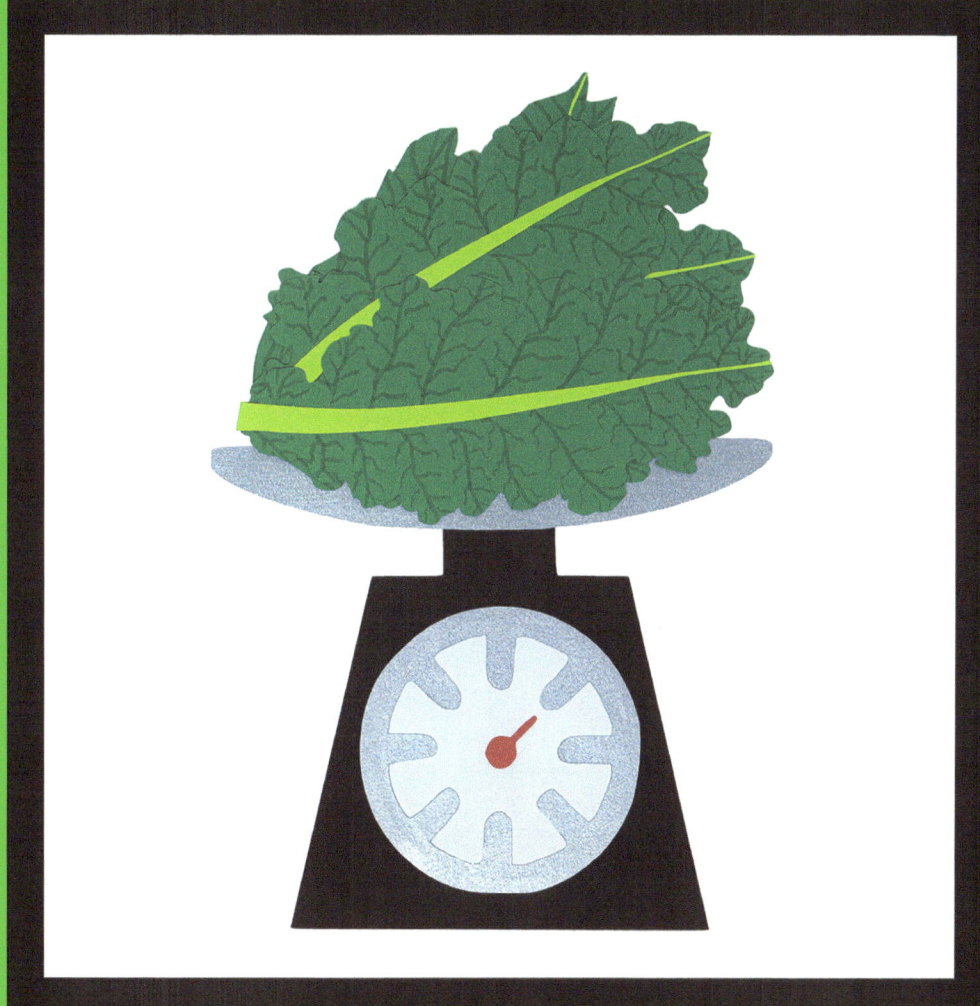

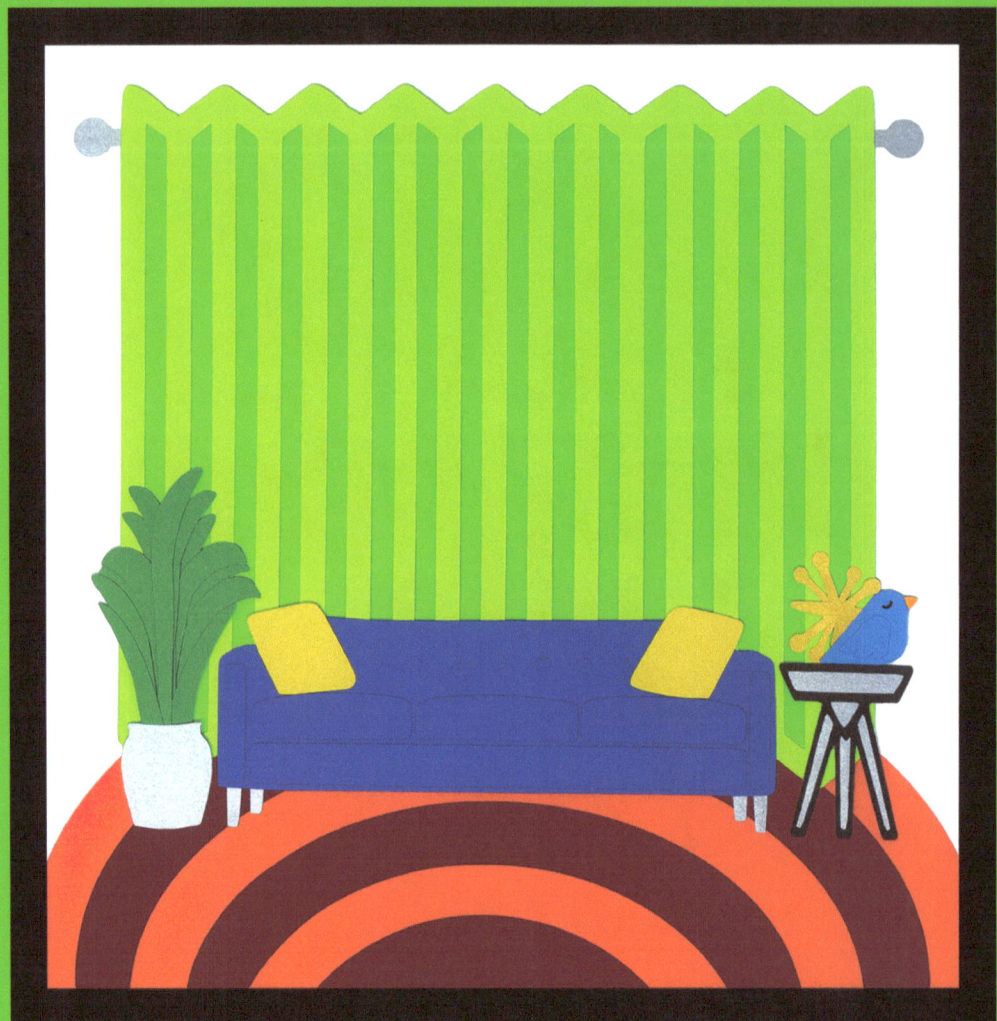

A GREEN GRAPE COLORED DRAPE...

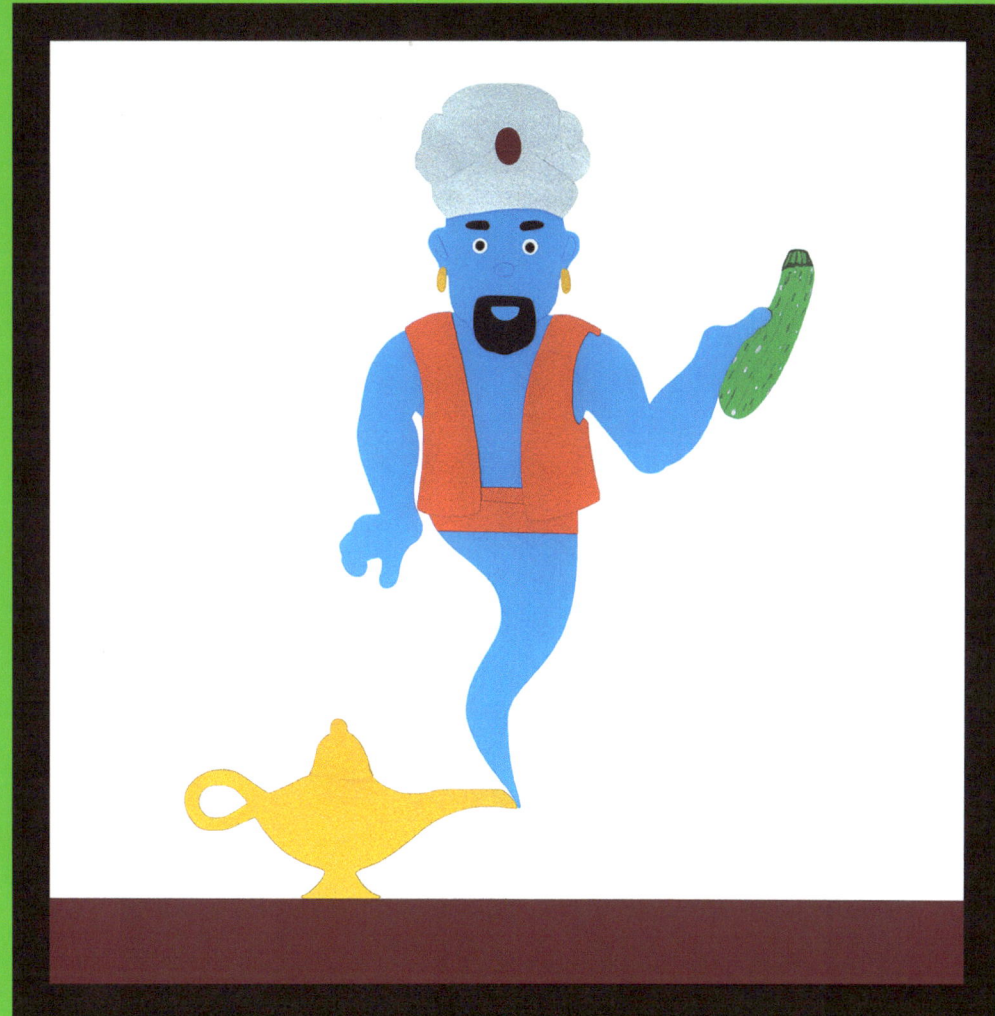

A GENIE HOLDING A ZUCCHINI...

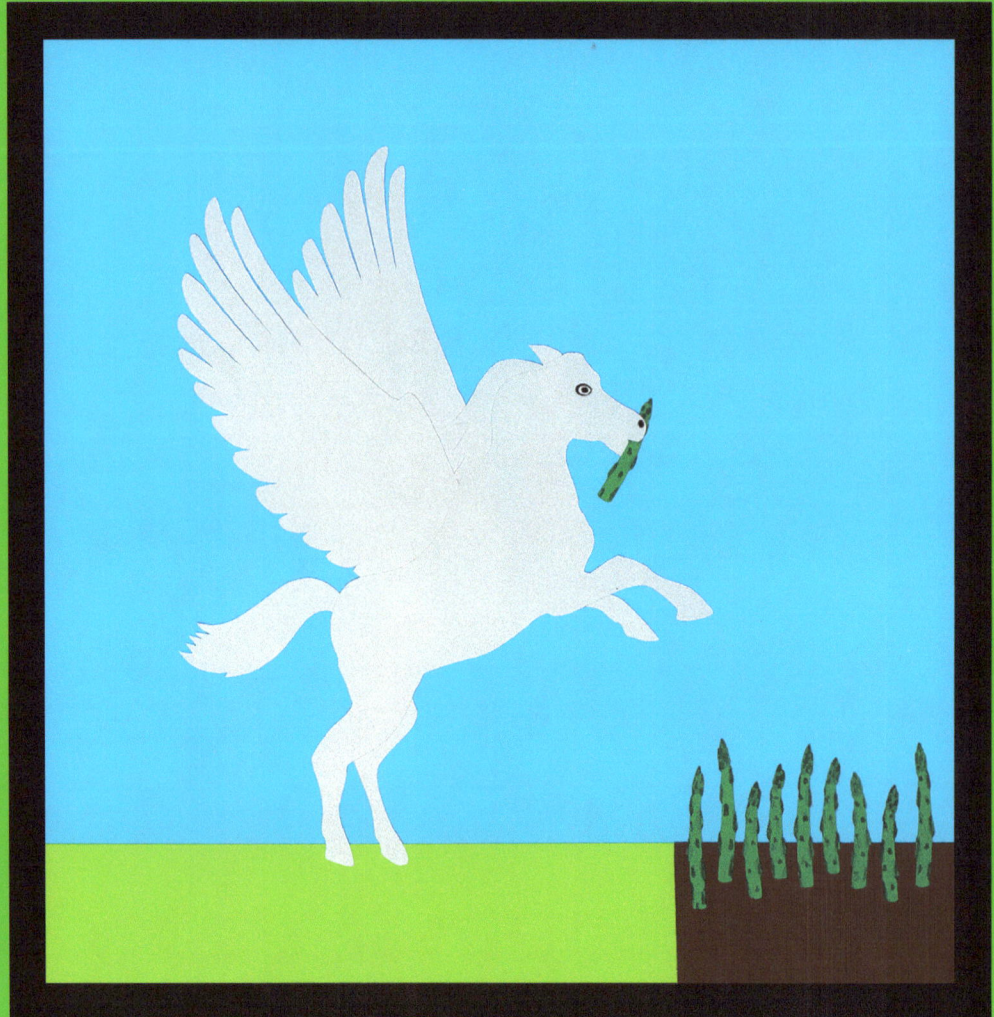

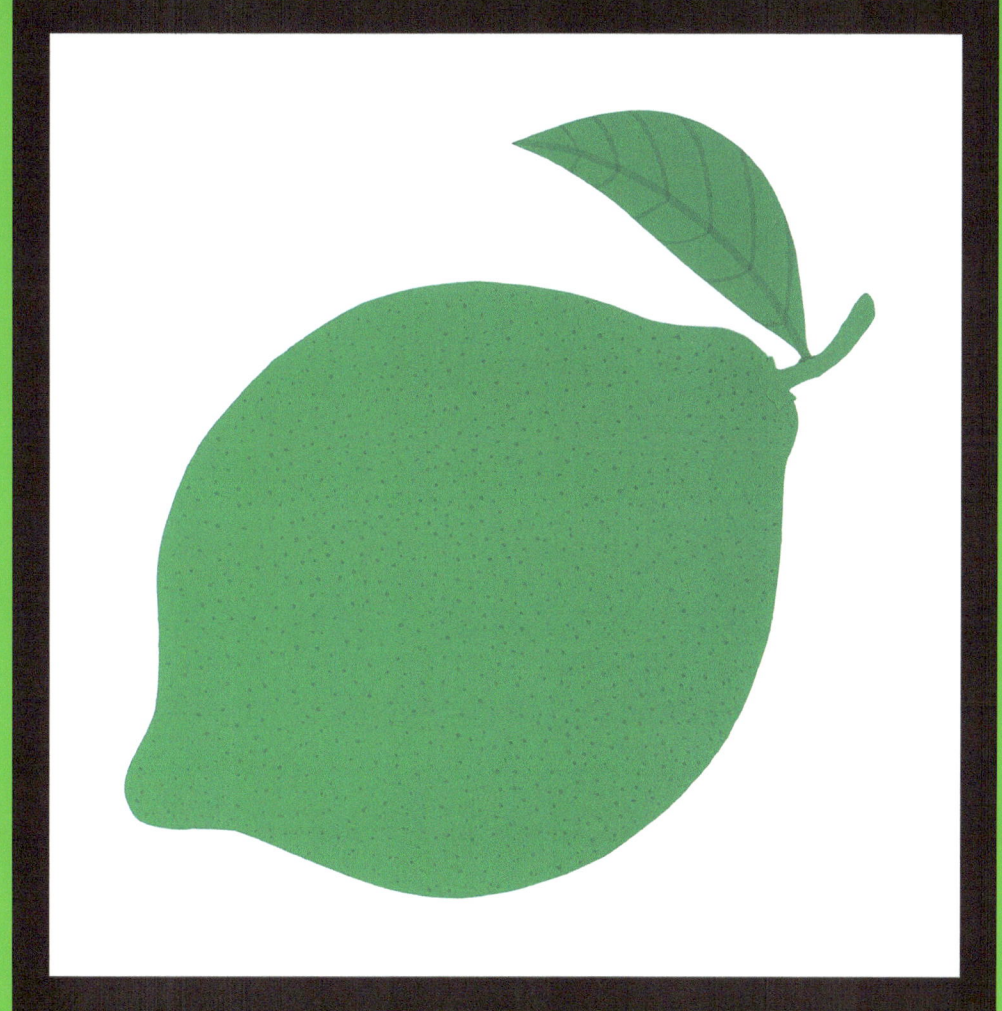

LET'S REVIEW EVERYTHING WE HAVE SEEN THAT IS GREEN!

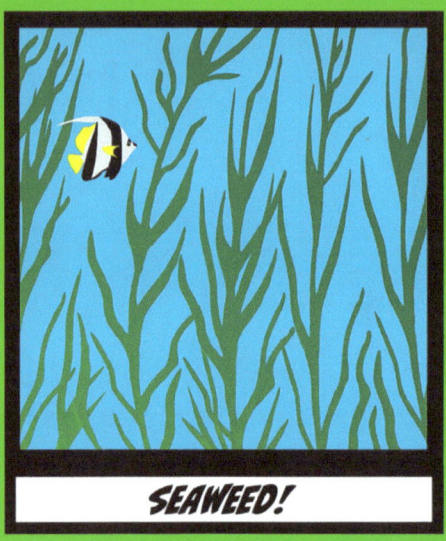

SEAWEED!

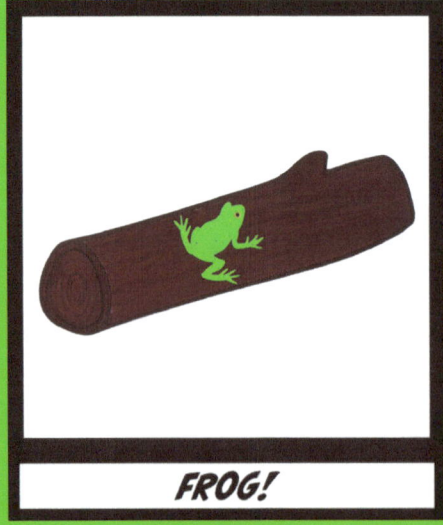

FROG!

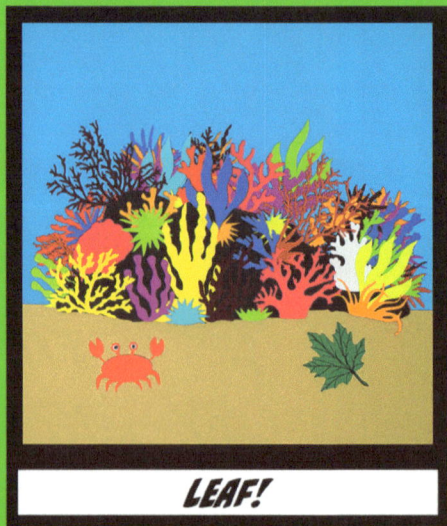

LEAF!

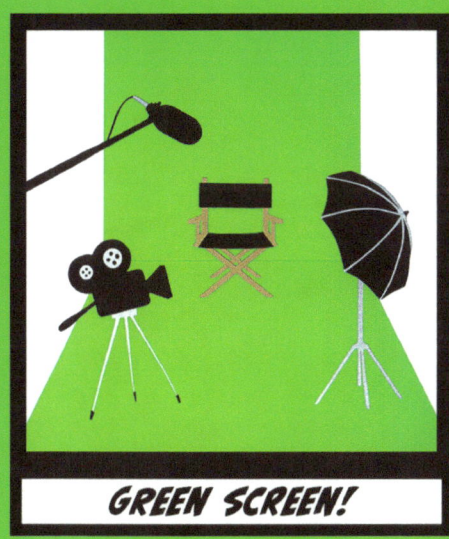
GREEN SCREEN!

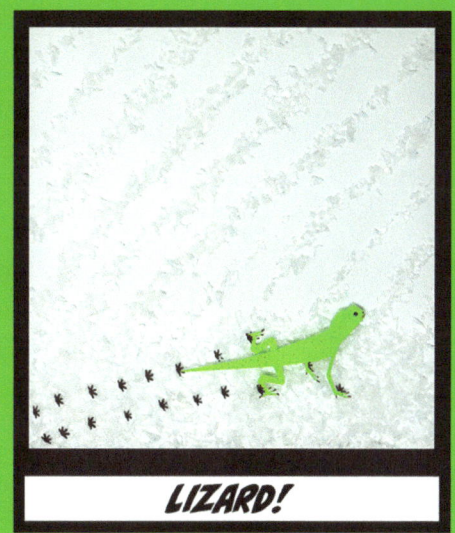
LIZARD!

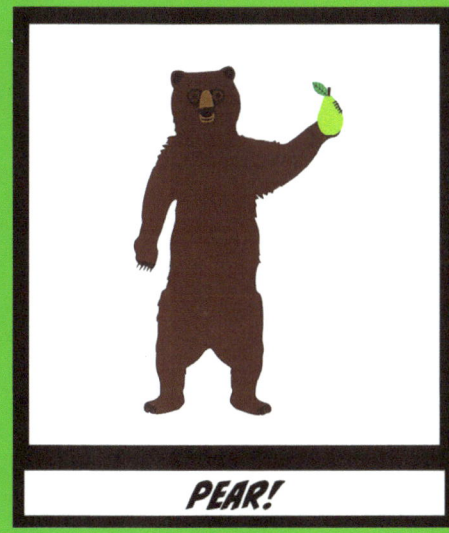
PEAR!

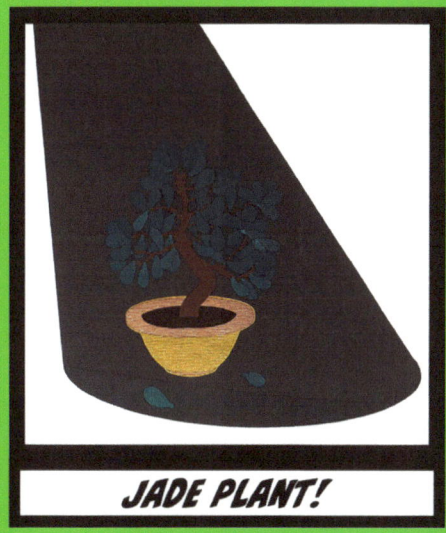
JADE PLANT!

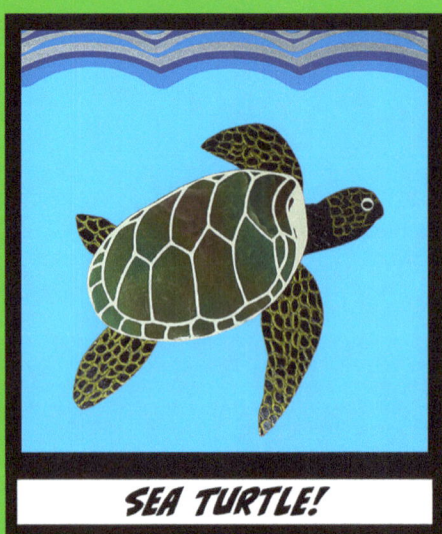
SEA TURTLE!

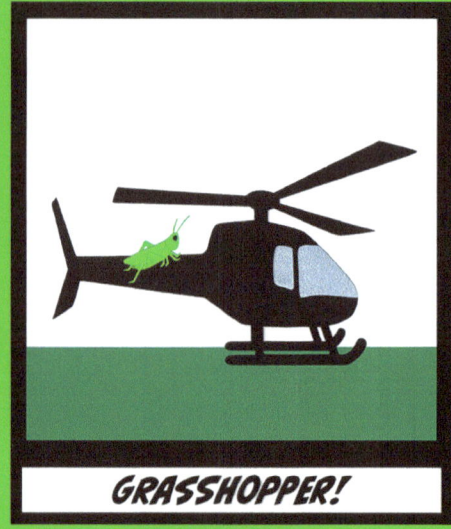
GRASSHOPPER!

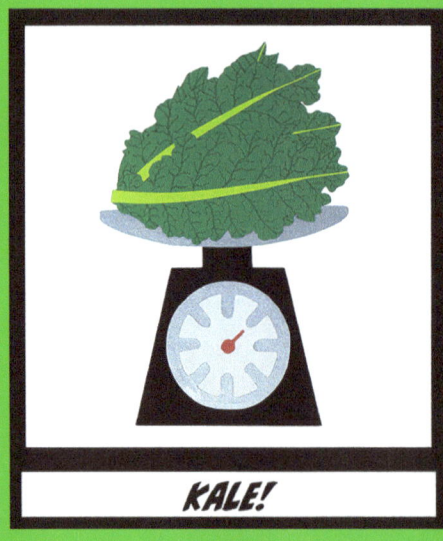
KALE!

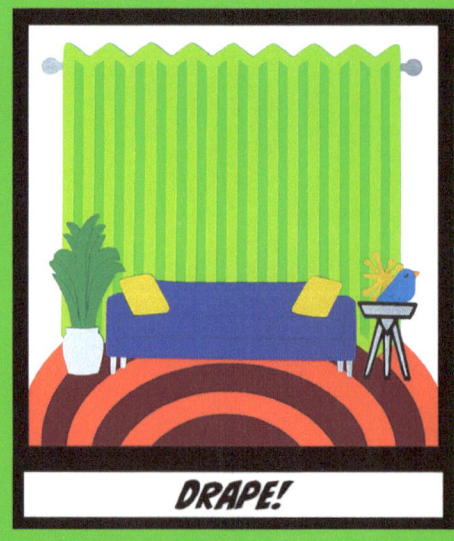
DRAPE!

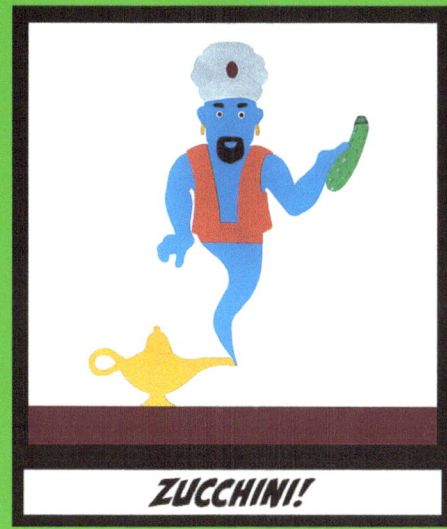

ZUCCHINI!

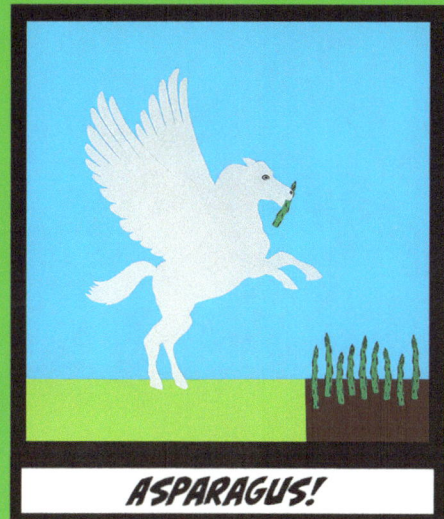

ASPARAGUS!

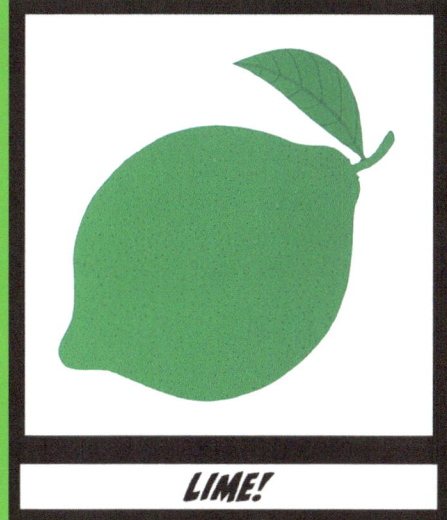

LIME!

NICE JOB, AND NOW WE'RE THROUGH. ISN'T IT FUN TO LEARN SOMETHING NEW!

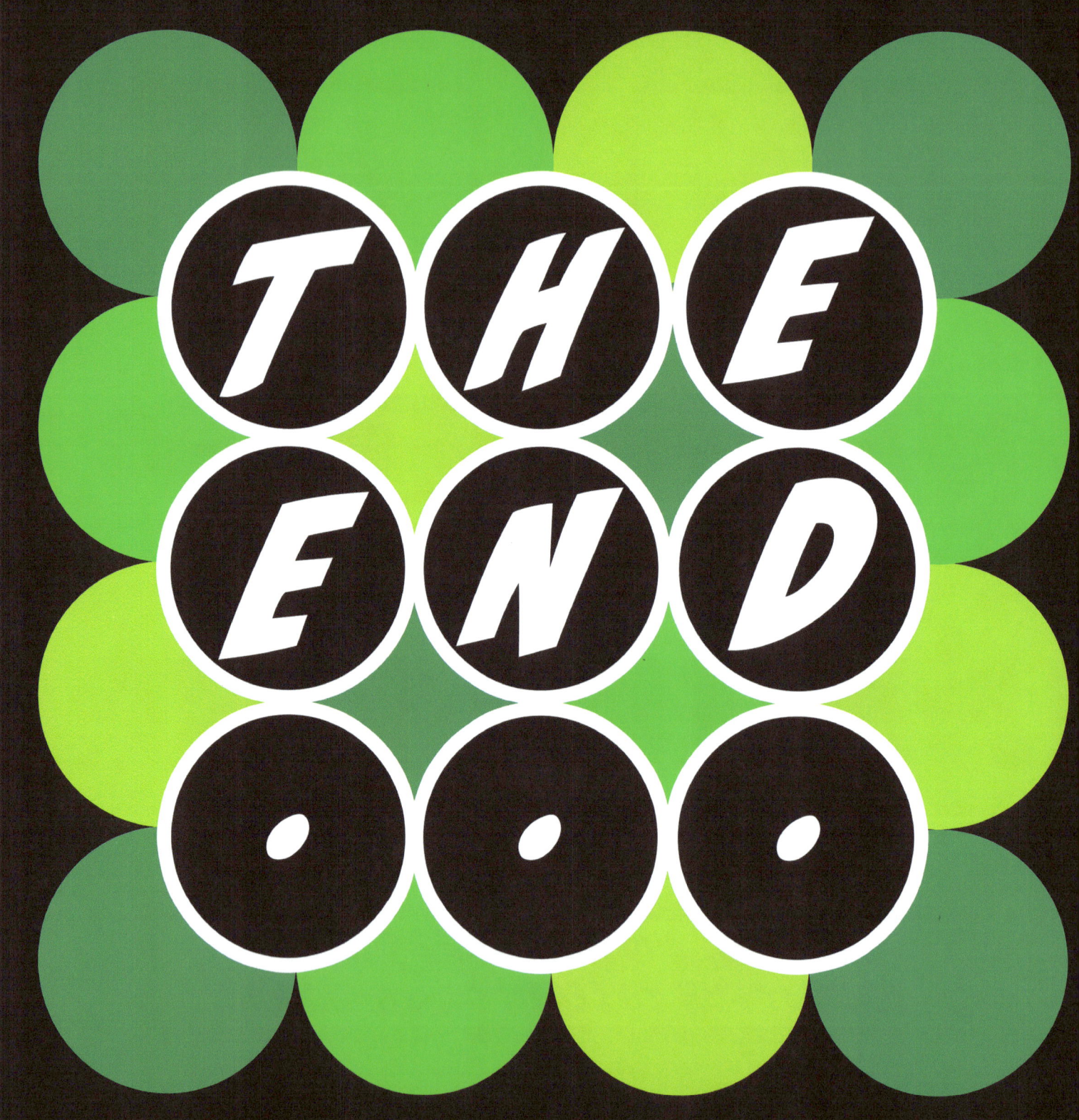

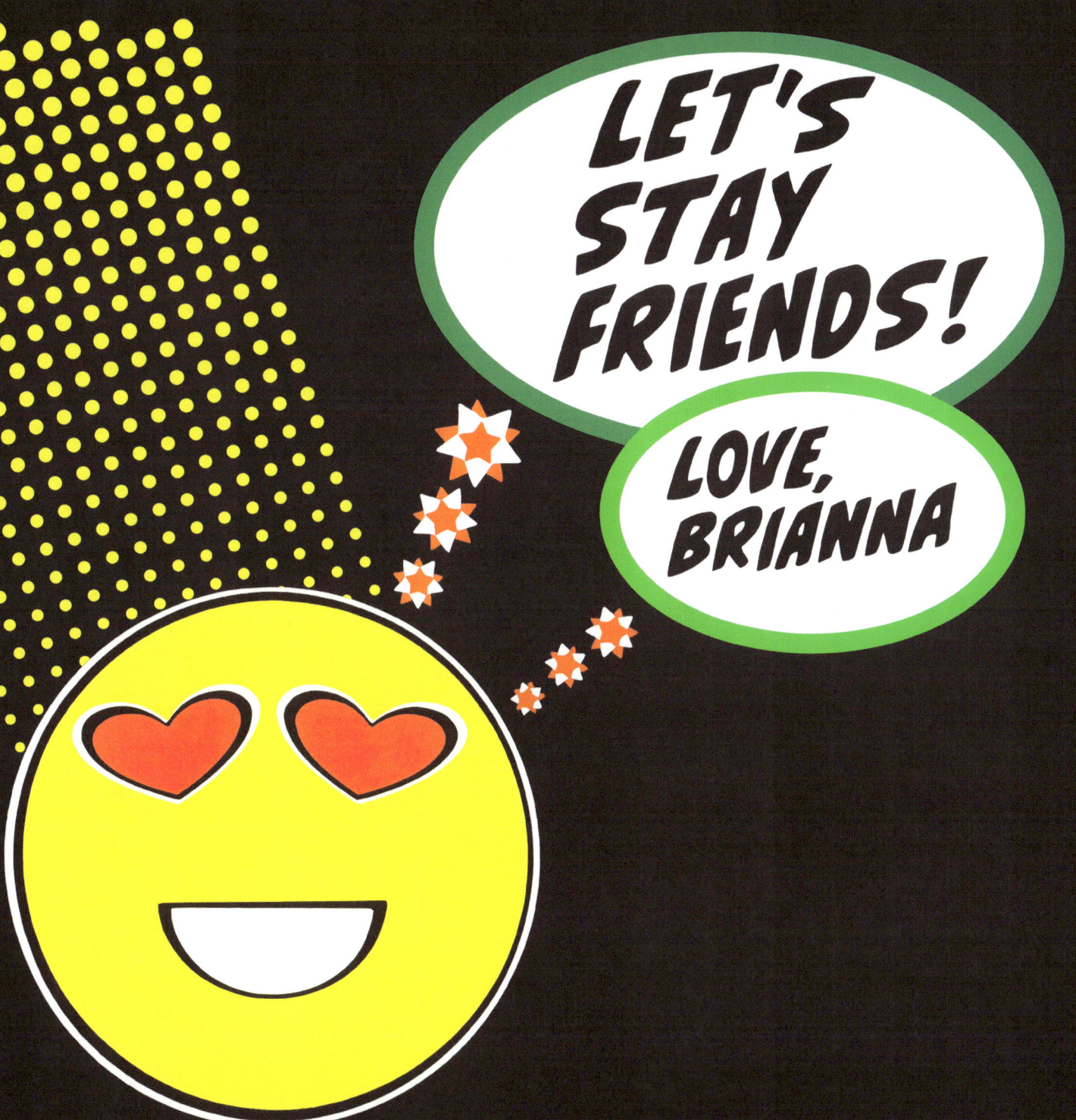

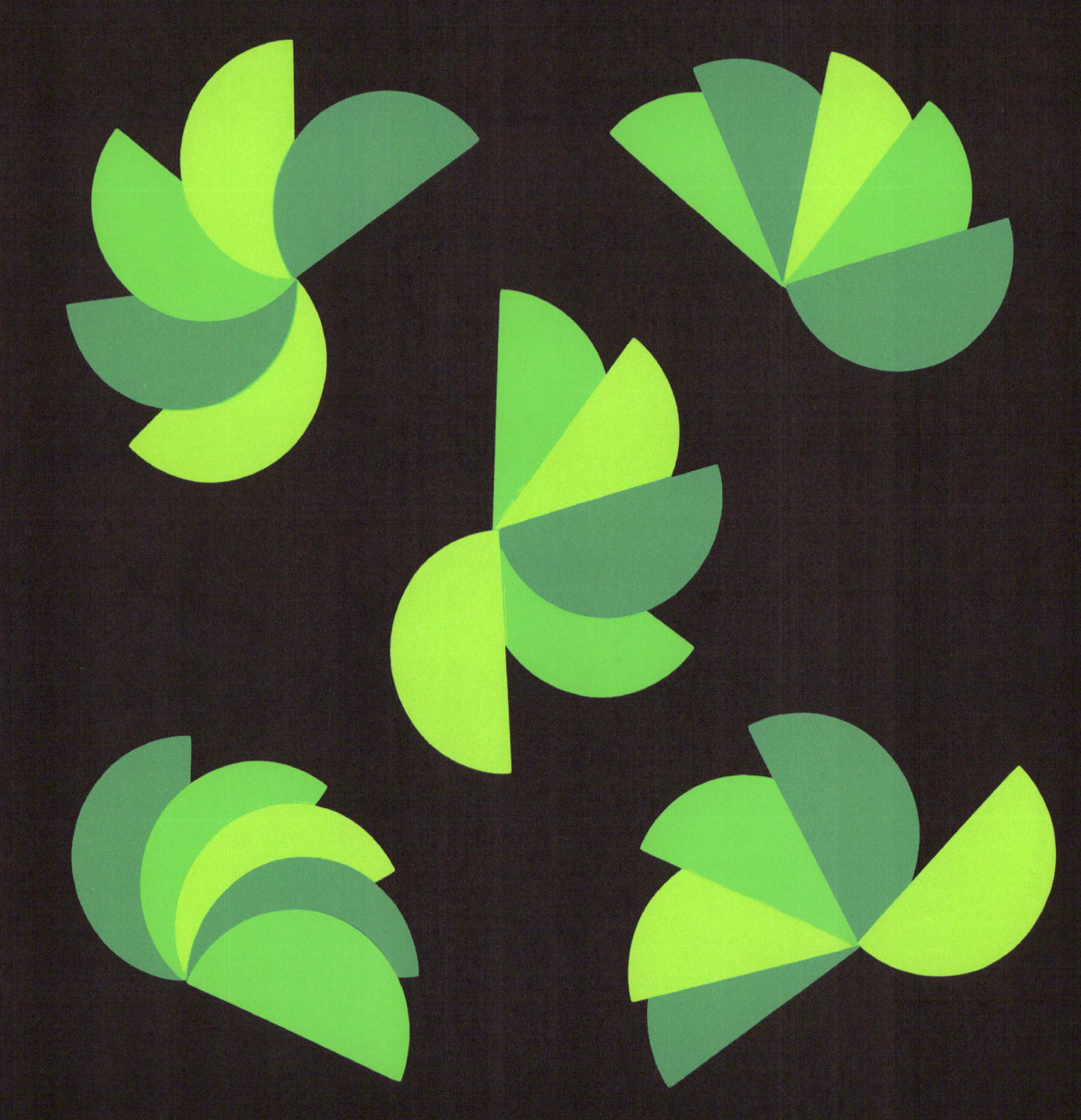

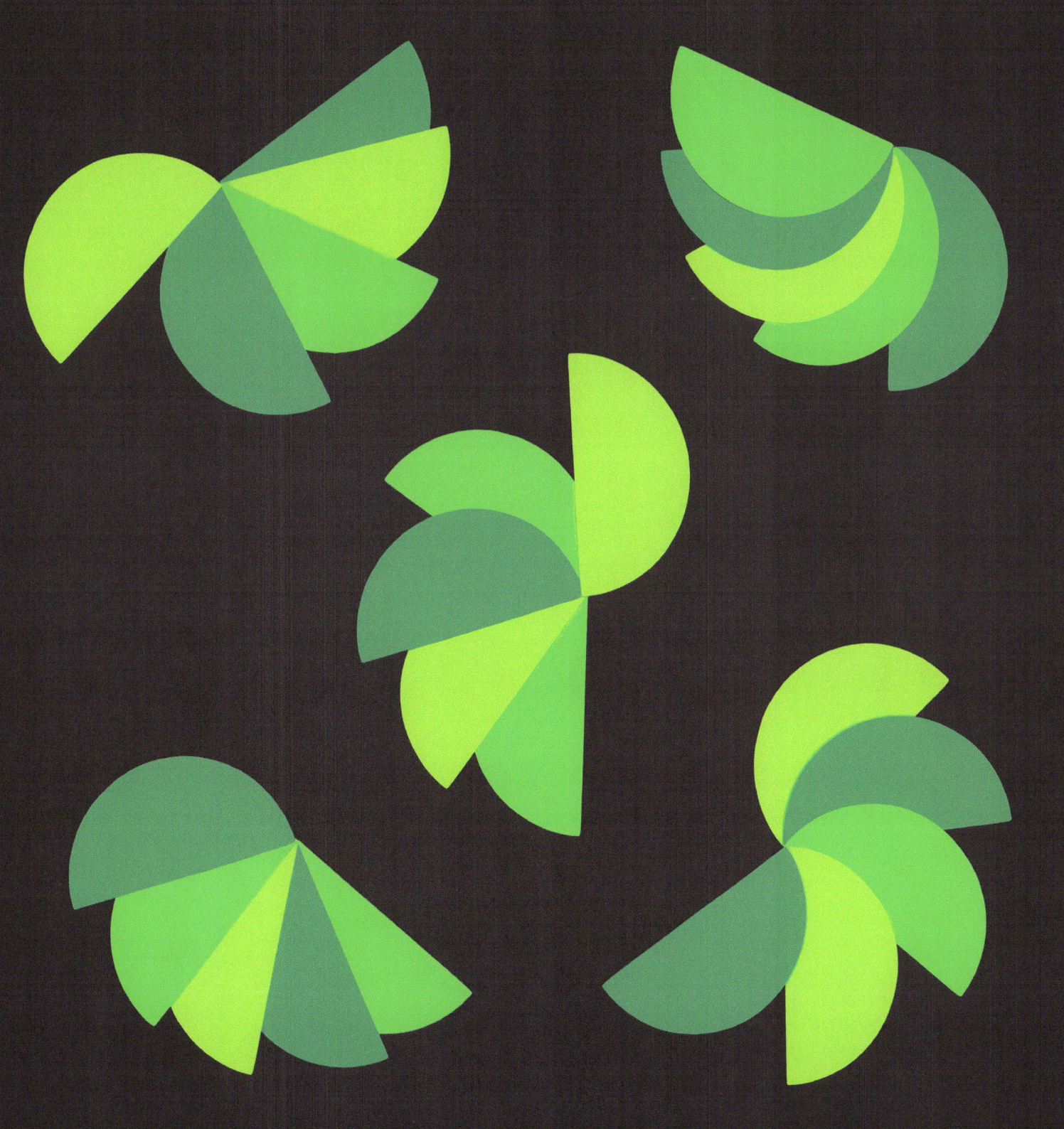

POP ART BOOKs
AVAILABLE NOW

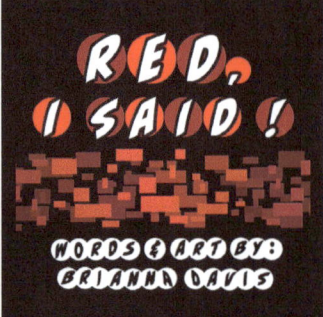
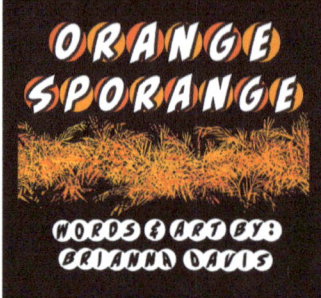
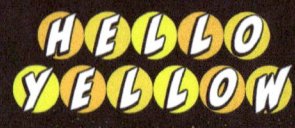
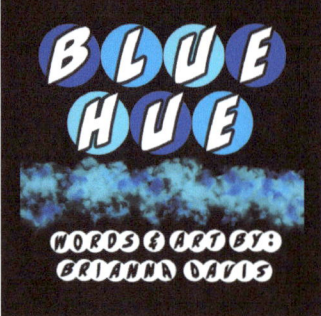
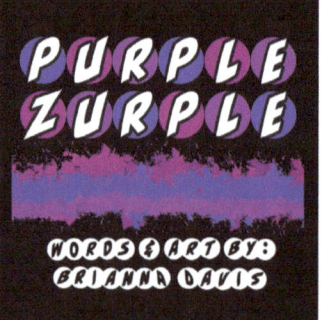
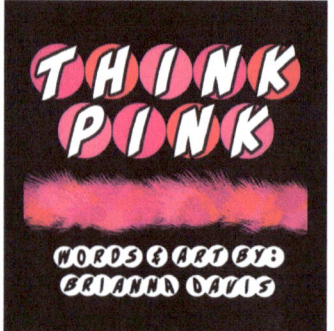
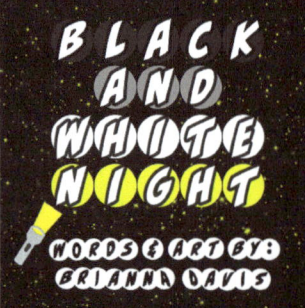
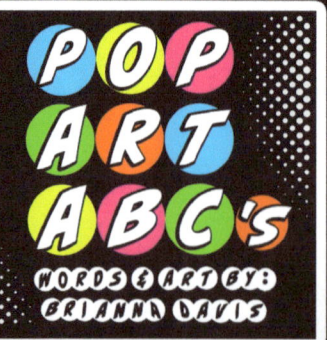
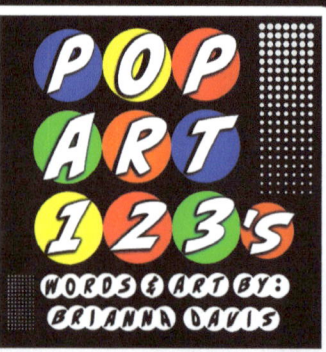

www.ingramcontent.com/pod-product-compliance
Lightning Source LLC
Chambersburg PA
CBHW051829210526
45473CB00005B/1802